Legendary Heroes

Contents

Written by Eva Wood

Introduction

What is a legendary hero, you may ask? Is it a movie star or a princess? Is it a person who is the best in the world at what they do? Or, is it someone who spends their life doing things that will help other people?

It is all of these. Legendary heroes are people who have made an impact on the lives of other people because of who they are and what they do. We all have heroes whom we respect and admire. Legendary heroes are people who are respected and admired by people all over the world.

Muhammad Ali

Muhammad Ali is one of the most famous athletes in the world.

Neil Armstrong

In 1969, the astronaut Neil Armstrong was the first person to walk on the moon.

Jacques Cousteau

Jacques Cousteau was a conservationist, author, and marine explorer.

Diana, Princess of Wales

Diana, Princess of Wales, brought world attention to problems faced by many poor people in third-world countries.

Mahatma Gandhi

Mahatma Gandhi was a great leader who did not believe in using violence.

Mother Teresa

Mother Teresa won a Nobel Peace Prize for her work helping the poor.

These are the stories of two legendary heroes. Although these two heroes seem very different, they have many qualities which are the same.

One was a great athlete. He was the best boxer in the world. Many years ago, he was often in the public eye. He talked a lot. He liked to be noticed. When he got older, however, he lived more quietly. He made a rare public appearance in 1996, in Atlanta, Georgia, where he lit the Olympic Flame, opening the Olympics.

Muhammad Ali

The other person never wanted to be noticed. She went quietly about her work of helping poor people in India. She lived with and cared for the homeless, the poor, and the dying. But she became very famous indeed for her work, and she inspired many other people to follow her example.

Mother Teresa

Mother Teresa

Agnes Gonxha Bojaxhiu was born in Skopje, Macedonia, in 1910. Her father was a businessman who was often away, and he died when Agnes was still a child. So Agnes's mother brought up her three children. She taught them to love those people who were not as well-off as they were.

Macedonia

Skopje

Europe

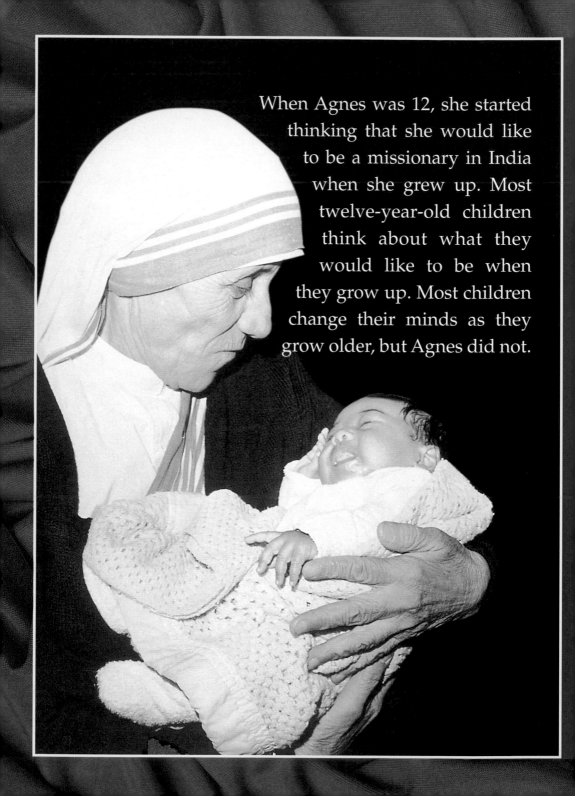

When Agnes was 12, she started thinking that she would like to be a missionary in India when she grew up. Most twelve-year-old children think about what they would like to be when they grow up. Most children change their minds as they grow older, but Agnes did not.

When Agnes was 18, she took the first step on the road to becoming a missionary. She left her family and went to Dublin, Ireland, to learn English and be trained in religious life.

By the end of 1928, Agnes was on a boat on her way to India. She went to Darjeeling, at the foot of the Himalayan mountains, to finish her religious training. It was here that she chose the name Teresa. After that, Sister Teresa, as Agnes was now known, went to Calcutta to learn to be a teacher.

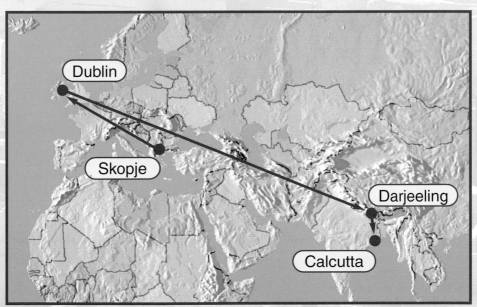

Time Line of Mother Teresa's Life

August 26, 1910 – Agnes Gonxha Bojaxhiu born in Skopje, Macedonia.

1928 – Joins a religious order. Goes to Dublin, Ireland. Learns to speak English and begins her religious training.

1929 – Goes to Darjeeling, at the foot of the Himalayas, to continue her religious training.

1929 – Teaches at a girls' school in Calcutta.

1948 – Granted permission to leave the order. Studies nursing. Begins teaching poor children in the Calcutta slums.

1910   1920   1930   1940   1950

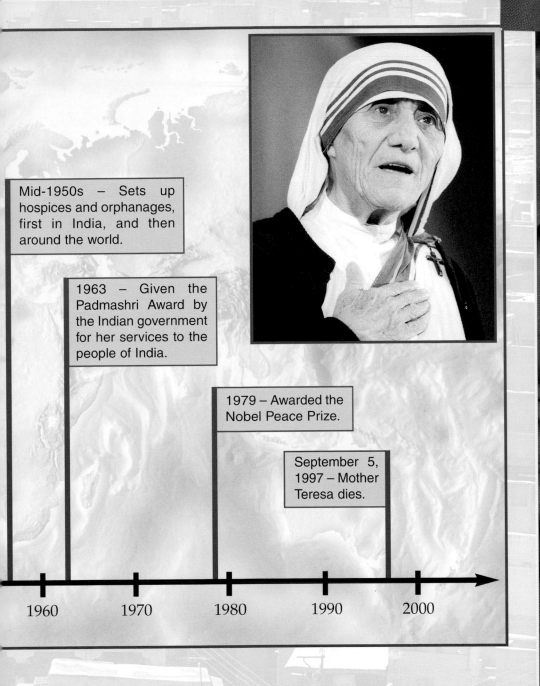

Mid-1950s – Sets up hospices and orphanages, first in India, and then around the world.

1963 – Given the Padmashri Award by the Indian government for her services to the people of India.

1979 – Awarded the Nobel Peace Prize.

September 5, 1997 – Mother Teresa dies.

1960   1970   1980   1990   2000

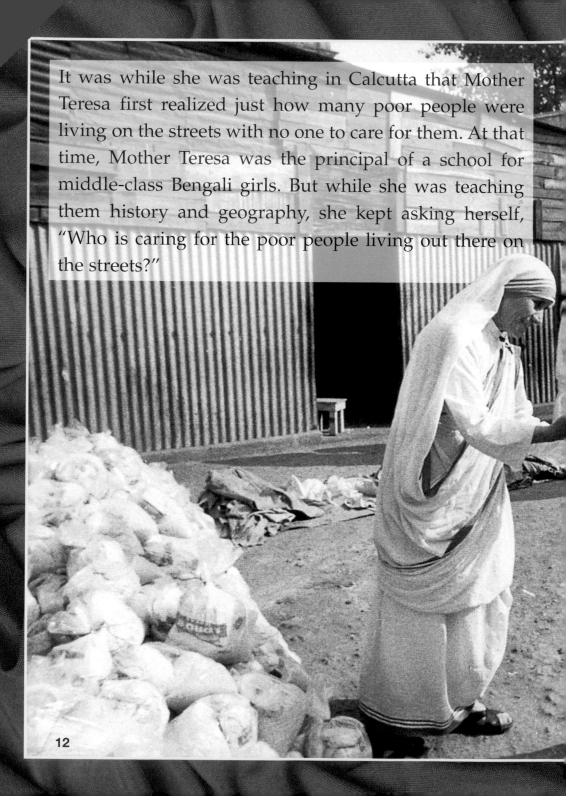

It was while she was teaching in Calcutta that Mother Teresa first realized just how many poor people were living on the streets with no one to care for them. At that time, Mother Teresa was the principal of a school for middle-class Bengali girls. But while she was teaching them history and geography, she kept asking herself, "Who is caring for the poor people living out there on the streets?"

Mother Teresa started thinking back to when she was 12. She had wanted to help the poor people in India, not teach well-off people's children. And that was still what she wanted to do. But to do it, she had to give up teaching and live and work among the poor.

But there were problems. India was about to become an independent country. It would no longer be a British colony, and it could become harder for Europeans to live there. Indian people might not like a European woman working among them. Mother Teresa would also need to get permission to leave the church order that she had joined. And where would the money to help the poor people come from?

Mother Teresa was determined and she did not give up her dream, although it took her many years to convince people that she could live and work with the poor people of Calcutta. In 1948, she trained to be a nurse so that she would know how to help people who were ill. Then, dressed in a plain white sari, with a piece of soap, and just five rupees, she started a school for the poor on the streets of Calcutta.

Prince Charles visited Mother Teresa's home for children.

In time, some of Mother Teresa's former students came to work with her. The very first one was from the middle-class school where Mother Teresa had taught when she first came to Calcutta. This girl changed her name to Agnes. And as Mother Teresa's group grew, they were able to help poor people in other cities, first in India, and then in other countries around the world.

Poor women in Calcutta

So, what makes Mother Teresa a legendary hero? She spent just about every day of her adult life caring for others. She cared for people who were poor, ill, dying, unwanted, and unloved. She fed them, sheltered them, and cleaned their wounds. She made them feel loved and good about themselves, even though they were poor.

When Mother Teresa died, world leaders attended her funeral.

Muhammad Ali

Born in 1942, in Louisville, Kentucky, Muhammad Ali is still one of the most recognizable people on Earth, even though he is now rarely in the public eye. But many years ago, he was one of the greatest athletes of all time.

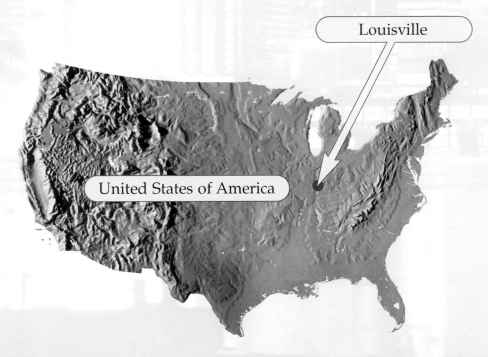

Louisville

United States of America

Muhammad Ali first became known to the world at the Olympic Games in Rome in 1960, where he won a gold medal for boxing. He was good at boxing. He was the best in the world, and he knew it. He often made up little poems to tell people how good he was. Part of one of his best-known poems that describes his style of fighting goes,

Float like a butterfly
Sting like a bee.

People who watched Muhammad Ali, known then as Cassius Clay, knew how true this little poem was. He was a big man, but he moved like a butterfly in the ring. He was always on his toes, moving this way and that to avoid punches. He did not only have speed, he had grace. Judging by the number of fights he won, his punch also stung like a bee.

After winning the gold medal at the Olympics in 1960, Muhammad Ali turned professional, and started beating the best boxers in the world. He told the world, "I am the greatest." And he was. By the time he retired from boxing in 1982, Muhammad Ali had won 56 fights. He had lost only five.

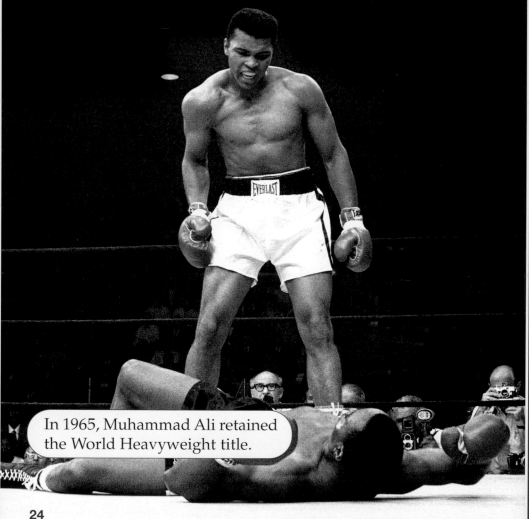

In 1965, Muhammad Ali retained the World Heavyweight title.

But it was not always this way. Muhammad Ali worked very hard to get to the top. He first learned to box when he was 12 years old. Someone had stolen his bicycle, and he was determined to find the person who had stolen it and fight them.

He never got his bicycle back. But by then he had already started to dream of being the heavyweight-boxing champion of the world. Right from the start, Muhammad Ali was determined to achieve his dream. He trained hard, six days a week. He won many competitions. And he got better and better at boxing, until he was the greatest in the world.

Muhammad Ali was the greatest boxer in the world.

There was another side to Muhammad Ali, the champion boxer. Like Mother Teresa, he had a faith that he followed. Like Mother Teresa, following that faith meant changing his name. So, he changed his name from Cassius Clay to Muhammad Ali.

Also like Mother Teresa, Muhammad Ali cared for all kinds of people, especially those poorer people living in third-world countries.

December 11, 1981
Lost to Trevor Berbick
Nassau, Bahamas

February 20, 1976
Won against Jean-Pierre Coopman
San Juan, Puerto Rico

One way Muhammad Ali could help those people was to fight world-championship fights in their countries. When he fought big fights in these countries, the world became aware of them. So he fought big fights in places like Manila, in the Philippines; Kuala Lumpur, in Malaysia; and Kinshasa, in Zaire (Zaire is now called the Democratic Republic of the Congo).

June 30, 1975
Won against Joe Bugner
Kuala Lumpur, Malaysia
(Retained World Heavyweight Title)

October 1, 1975
Won against Joe Frazier
Manila, Philippines
(Retained World Heavyweight Title)

October 30, 1974
Won against George Foreman
Kinshasa, Zaire
(Democratic Republic of the Congo)
(Won World Heavyweight Title)

October 20, 1973
Won against Rudi Lubbers
Jakarta, Indonesia

And because Muhammad Ali was a world champion and also an African-American, other African-American people felt proud of him, and felt more pride in themselves, too.

Many African-American people felt proud of Muhammad Ali.

Legendary Heroes

So what is it that makes Mother Teresa and Muhammad Ali legendary heroes? At first glance, they seem so different. One was a sports hero, the other was a worker for the poor. But a closer look will show you the things they have in common. Mother Teresa and Muhammad Ali believed in themselves and helped others. They both had dreams that they made happen through their own courage, confidence, and determination.

Qualities of a Legendary Hero

confidence

self -belief

not being stopped by setbacks

having a purpose

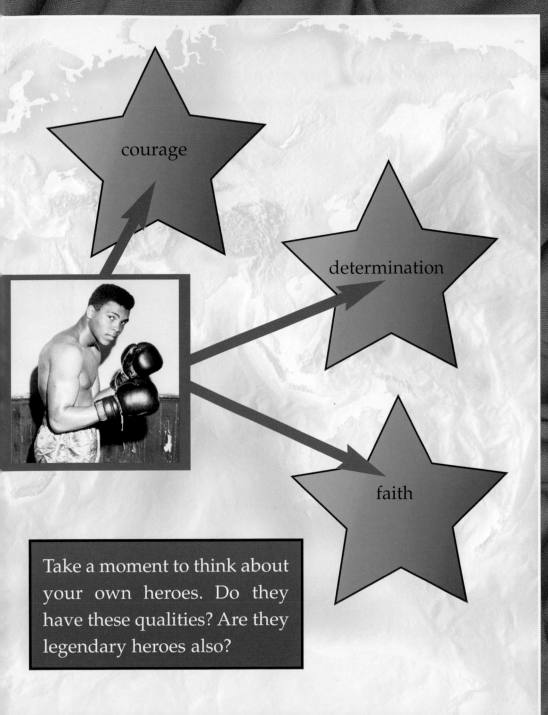

courage

determination

faith

Take a moment to think about your own heroes. Do they have these qualities? Are they legendary heroes also?

Glossary

colony – A territory distant from the state having control over it. India was a British colony from about 1750 until 1947.

impact – A strong effect or influence.

legendary – Remarkable enough to be famous.

missionary – A person sent on a religious mission. A missionary is usually sent to places where the people are very poor.

professional – A person who makes a living from an activity, such as playing a sport.

qualities – The features or characteristics that make someone what he or she is.

rupees – The basic monetary unit of India.

sari – The traditional garment worn by women in India and Pakistan.